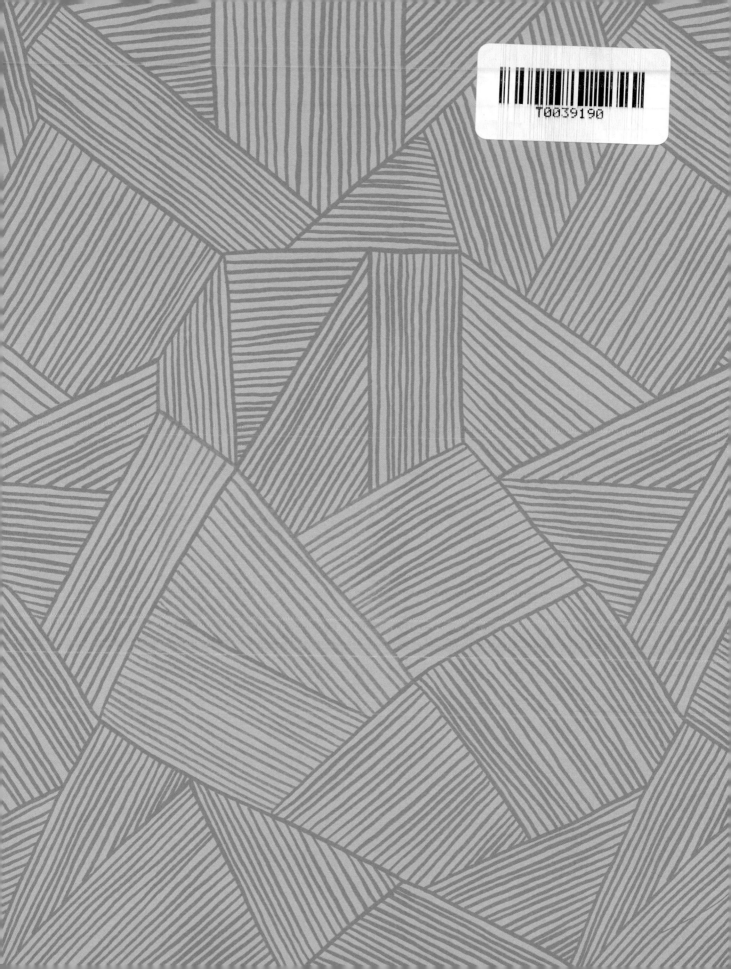

Louise Bourgeois

She saw the world as a textured tapestry

Written by
Amy Guglielmo

Illustrated by
Katy Knapp

On Christmas Day 1911,
Louise Joséphine Bourgeois
was born in an apartment
above a café in Paris, France.

Her parents, Joséphine
and Louis, found and
repaired old tapestries
and sold them in
their gallery.

Soon after Louise was born, the First World War began, and her father was sent to fight. The family rented a house just outside of Paris. Behind the elegant, white house, her parents set up a two-story workshop and hired workers to restore the tattered, thread-worn tapestries. Louise spent time in the gardens and in the studio watching the weavers at work.

To keep safe as the war went on, the family also spent time at Louise's grandparents' house in Aubusson. Louise's mother had learned the tapestry trade here, passed down through her family for generations.

When the war ended, Louise's parents bought a grand, spacious house in the town of Antony, just outside of Paris. The property had a large tapestry studio and fancy gardens that led to the banks of the Bièvre River.

There, the roots of the plants that grew along the riverbanks created a chemical called tannin that helped set the colors for dying tapestry wool. Louise played by the water where she watched the laundresses wash the tapestries on the riverbank. She saw the women boil large pots of dye inside and then hang the colorful skeins of wool to dry in the garden.

In the garden, Louise also collected rocks, tended fruit trees, and camped with her sister and brother in a fabric tent. At night in the tent, Louise listened to the murmuring river, gazed at the stars, and learned not to fear the dark.

As Louise grew older, she often helped care for her mother, who had never fully recovered after catching the Spanish flu at the end of the war. The family spent every winter in the South of France, where the warmer climate was better for her mother's health.

One day, when a worker didn't show up, Louise's mother asked Louise to help in the studio. Since she was fond of drawing, Louise's job was to fill in the bottom part of the design, the part of the tapestry that often had the most wear.

Many of the tapestries were covered in scenes of biblical and mythological figures, so Louise soon became an expert at drawing feet. She also learned how to mend, dye, weave, and sew. She started keeping a diary of her inner thoughts.

When she was a little older, Louise took drawing classes and studied piano. She loved mathematics and learned about calculus and geometry. Numbers, formulas, and equations filled her brain.

Louise enjoyed math because it was a subject that had order. She had yearned for a sense of stability, and math gave it to her.

But then her mother died, and Louise felt alone and abandoned.

Louise was very sad about her mother's death. She soon quit studying math and switched to art instead. She studied drawing, painting, and sculpture at the École des Beaux-Arts and the Académie de la Grande Chaumière, and took art history courses at the École du Louvre. To help pay for her classes, she worked as a teaching assistant and museum guide at the Musée du Louvre.

Have you ever visited a museum or gallery?

What did you see?

At that time, many artists in Paris opened their own studios and taught classes. Louise studied with different artists this way, including the famous cubist painter Fernand Léger. He was the first to recognize her as a sculptor, telling her, "You are not a painter. You are a sculptor."

In 1936, Louise exhibited her artwork for the first time in Paris. In 1938, she opened her own gallery in a section of her father's tapestry gallery and sold drawings and prints by other artists, such as Picasso.

There, she met an American art historian named Robert Goldwater. They fell in love, and not long after, they were married. Robert returned to America, and soon Louise joined him. They were both excited to start their life together in New York.

Louise found New York City loud, crowded, and busy, but the energy of the city inspired her. She was amazed by the towering skyscrapers, the gritty, congested streets, and the bright blue sky.

Louise took classes at the Art Students League and learned how to make prints. She and Robert socialized with other artists who had left Europe, as well as American artists and important collectors and dealers from the New York art scene.

New York was booming, building, and growing, and so was Louise's family. In 1939, she and her husband adopted a child from France. Then later Louise gave birth to two more sons.

Where would you would like to travel?

What do you think you would see *there?*

Despite her many responsibilities, Louise continued to make art. Her painting of a woman's body with a house for a head, *Femme Maison*, was included in a solo exhibition. She also experimented with carving sculptures out of wood on the roof of her apartment building.

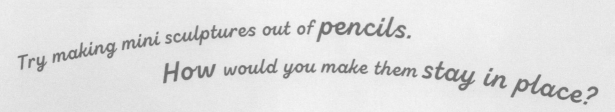

Try making mini sculptures out of **pencils**. **How** would you make them **stay in place?**

In 1949, Louise was given her first solo sculpture show, where she displayed carved wooden poles. Louise had not been able to return to France for a long time because of the Second World War, and the sculptures represented the people whom she missed from home. They were arranged to look like people talking at a party.

When Louise's father died unexpectedly in 1951, she was heartbroken. She worked through her feelings with a therapist, who encouraged her to explore her emotions through writing. During this time, she did not produce many works of art. Occasionally, she exhibited in group shows, and some of her work sold. For a brief time, she opened a small bookstore and sold books and prints.

As her spirits began to lift, Louise tried new materials and forms.
Switching from her previous work with hard materials like wood,
Louise used softer materials like plaster, latex, and rubber to create
molded organic sculptures. She referred to many of these new forms
as "Lairs" and explained that, like an animal's lair or a bird's nest,
they were safe hiding spaces.

In 1964, Louise had her first solo show of new work in 11 years. Two years later, several of her pieces were chosen to be displayed in a groundbreaking show along with a new generation of young artists. There was renewed interest in her work.

Then, Louise began traveling to Italy to learn about working in marble and bronze. She shaped the hard materials until they looked like fabric. She soon became known for her use of curvy, soft shapes that echoed the female form. Throughout the 1970s, Louise participated in demonstrations and exhibitions connected with the feminist movement, supporting women's rights.

In 1973, Louise was awarded a grant from the National Endowment for the Arts. Things were going well! But then her husband, Robert, died, and Louise poured her emotions into her work. Living alone for the first time, she transformed her whole house into a studio.

In 1978, she put on a mock fashion show with models wearing bulbous costumes. She molded the costumes out of latex, which made them look like skin.

Put on a **fashion show!**

How could you use old clothes in *new ways?*

Louise found a larger studio in
an old garment factory in Brooklyn.
This new space allowed her to work
on an even grander scale.

In 1982, Louise was given a show at the Museum of Modern Art to recognize the development of her work over her entire career. It was the first show given to a woman sculptor in the museum's history.

In a video she made for the show, Louise presented photos from her childhood. She spoke about how her past influenced her art.

It was around this time that Louise met Jerry Gorovoy. They became close friends, and he worked as her assistant for the next 30 years.

In 1990, Louise discovered glass cupping jars at a flea market that reminded her of the ones she had placed on her mother's back when she was sick. She made a sculpture with them, placing them on a slab of gray marble and lighting them from within. Soon, she was recycling more found objects and items from her past into new sculptures.

In 1993, Louise represented the United States at the American Pavilion at the Venice Biennale in Italy. Since 1895, the exhibition has been held every two years to bring attention to working artists around the world.

Do you keep treasures from the past?
What do they remind you of?

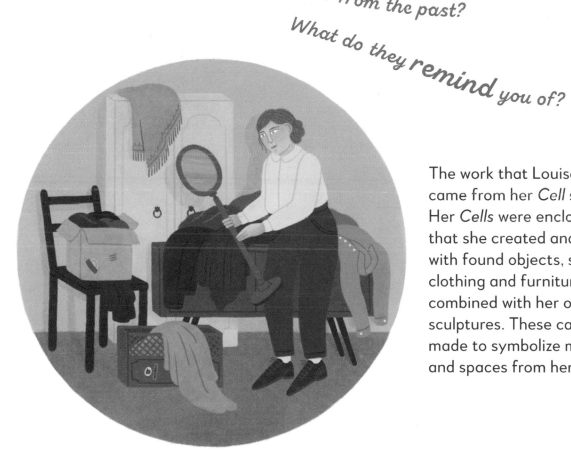

The work that Louise included came from her *Cell* series. Her *Cells* were enclosures that she created and filled with found objects, such as clothing and furniture, combined with her own sculptures. These cages were made to symbolize memories and spaces from her life.

Throughout her life, Louise had trouble sleeping.
In the silence of the night, she drew to relax
and eventually fall back to sleep. In this way,
her drawings were a kind of lullaby to herself.

Between November 1994 and June 1995, Louise completed
a series of 220 drawings, scribbles, and notes, filled with
wavy lines, spirals and patterns, houses, plants, and trees.
The *Insomnia Drawings* captured her feelings,
memories, and thoughts on paper.

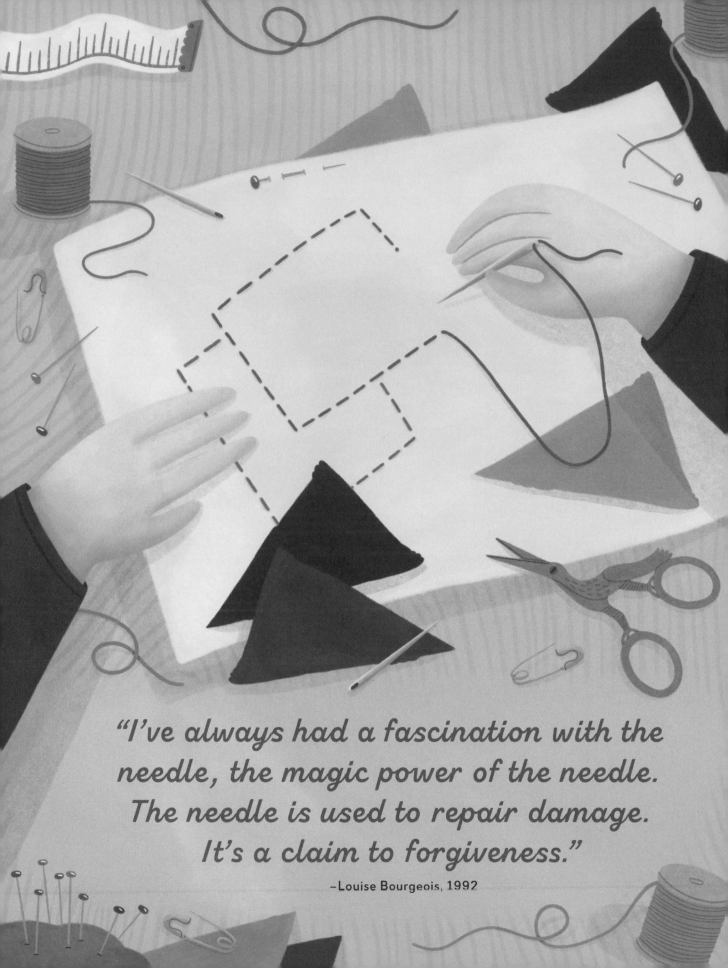

"I've always had a fascination with the needle, the magic power of the needle. The needle is used to repair damage. It's a claim to forgiveness."

–Louise Bourgeois, 1992

Do you have clothes that remind you of a special day or person?

Since she was a child, Louise had been around needles and thread. Fabric and sewing became a central focus of her sculptural work in the mid-1990s. Using clothing from her past to recreate memories, she printed on old handkerchiefs, hung her old dresses and nightgowns in arrangements, and constructed stuffed fabric figures. She also made books of fabric collages. She gave new life to clothes from her past.

In the mid-1990s, Louise began creating her most famous works of art, her iconic spider sculptures. *Maman*, French for "mom," was the name of the largest of these. At 30 feet high, it towered over viewers in locations around the globe. Louise thought of spiders as nurturing, creative guardians, like her mother. Her spiders were also a sort of self-portrait. Spiders spin webs from their own bodies, just like Louise made art from her inner emotions.

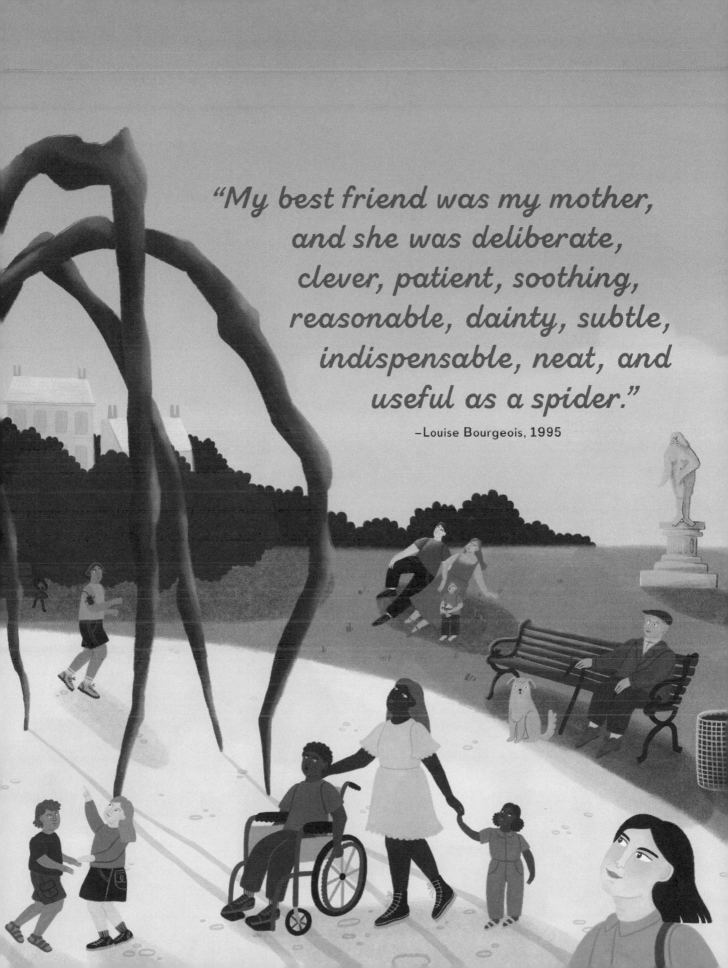

"My best friend was my mother, and she was deliberate, clever, patient, soothing, reasonable, dainty, subtle, indispensable, neat, and useful as a spider."

—Louise Bourgeois, 1995

In addition to her sculptures of spiders, Louise made spider drawings and prints. The print *Spider Woman* shows an image of a human face placed on a spider's body, in Louise's signature red ink. Louise's legendary spider-themed art made her known around the world.

In 1997, Louise was to be presented the National Medal of Arts by President Clinton at the White House. No longer interested in leaving her studio, she sent her son Jean-Louis to collect the award in her honor.

LOUISE BOURGEOIS

In 1999, Louise was invited to participate in the 48th Venice Biennale with six of her fabric works. She was awarded the Golden Lion prize for a living master of contemporary art.

In her later years, Louise stopped attending most events, letting her art speak for her in galleries, public spaces, and museums. She continued to work with Jerry Gorovoy. He helped with the installation of her sculptures, which were bold and monumental.

What would it be like to **create art** with a *friend*?
How would you **help** each other?

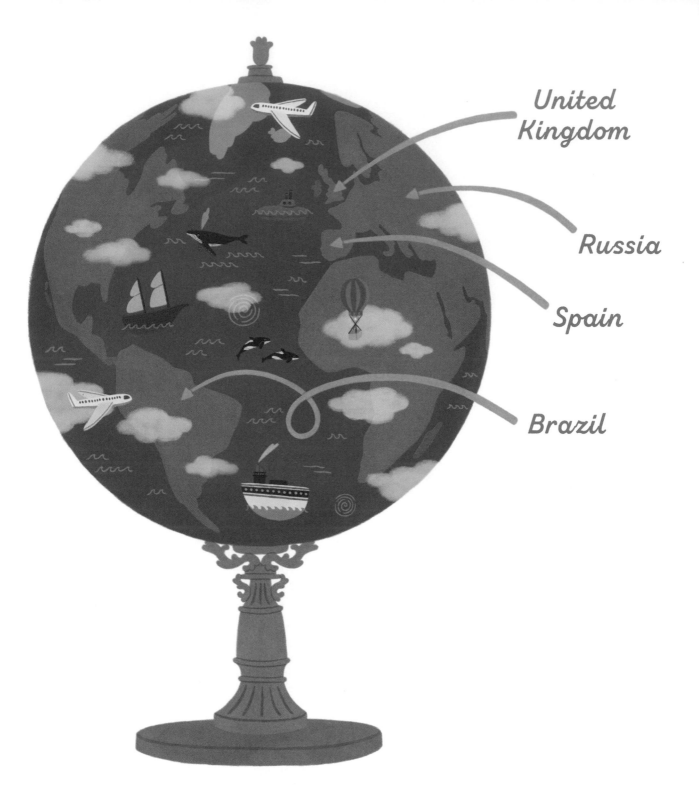

United Kingdom

Russia

Spain

Brazil

Even though she was at home in her studio, working, repairing, building, and sewing, her pictures, sculptures, and creations took her to places near and far. Her work traveled to Brazil, the United Kingdom, Spain, and Russia.

Love was an important theme in Louise's work. In 2010, she created the piece *I Do*. It depicted two flowers growing from one stem. She donated this piece to an organization that campaigned for marriage equality.

"Everyone should have the right to marry. To make a commitment to love someone forever is a beautiful thing."

–Louise Bourgeois, 2010

In May of that year, Louise died in New York City.

For more than 70 years, Louise Bourgeois made her mark on modern and contemporary art. From an early age, when she learned the traditional techniques of weaving and sewing from her mother, to her later years, she continued to grow and challenge herself through her art.

Never giving up, always testing new materials and methods, she constantly reimagined and reinvented her style. Her work continues to influence contemporary artists today.

Louise spent decades weaving her own tapestry of memories into her work and bringing them to life.

"I have kept a diary as long as I can remember, and drawings are another kind of diary."

–Louise Bourgeois, 2009

Timeline of key artworks

During her 70-year career, Louise Bourgeois produced prints, paintings, sculptures, installations, and fabric art. Here are a few of her works, some of which can be found in the collection of The Metropolitan Museum of Art.

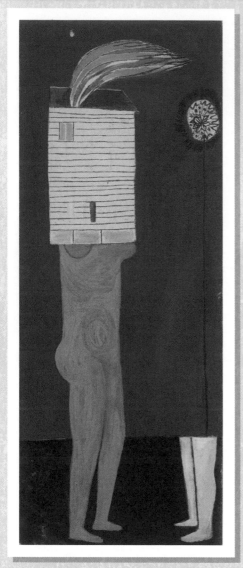

1946-47
Femme Maison
Oil and ink on linen

1968
*The Sweet Smell
of Indigo*
Watercolor, charcoal,
and gouache on paper

"Everything I do was
inspired by my early life."
–Louise Bourgeois, 1982

1982 *Eyes*
Marble

"The spider is a repairer.
If you bash into the web
of a spider, she doesn't
get mad. She weaves
and repairs it."
–Louise Bourgeois, 1998

1998 *Three Horizontals*
Fabric and steel

1999 *Maman*
Bronze, marble, and
stainless steel

2005 *Spider Woman*
Drypoint

Spider with a face

At various points in her career, Louise used the image of spiders in drawings, prints, and sculptures. She used them to represent her mother and the protective nature of spiders.

"Tell your own story, and you will be interesting."

–Louise Bourgeois, 2008

Using your favorite color, try to create a drawing of a spider with a human face.

Who will you choose to draw for the face? Will you draw a friend, a pet, or yourself? When an artist makes an image of themselves it is called a self-portrait. After you complete the face, add long, hairy spider legs to the portrait and enclose the spider in an egg shape.

Create your own version!

For a different challenge, add your face to an animal that you feel represents you.

Stuffed doll

As a child in her family's tapestry studio, Louise became familiar with sewing and working with fabric. Fabric became the focus of her sculptural work in the 1990s. Using clothing from her past to recreate memories, she printed on old handkerchiefs, hung her dresses and nightgowns in arrangements, and constructed stuffed figures.

Try this yourself!

Using a scrap of old clothing or a stray sock, create a stuffed face or doll. You can ask an adult for help using a needle and thread. Search for found objects like buttons, yarn, or other materials to add for eyes, nose, and mouth.

"Clothing is ... an exercise in memory. It makes me explore the past: how did I feel when I wore that? They are like signposts in the search for the past."

–Louise Bourgeois, 1997

Glossary

atelier *(noun)*
Workshop, studio

contemporary art *(noun)*
Artwork made during the late 20th and early 21st centuries

critic *(noun)*
A person who judges the merits of a work of art

exhibition *(noun)*
A public display of works of art or other items of interest

feminist movement *(noun)*
The fight for women's equality and rights

gallery *(noun)*
A building or room that features works of art for show or sale

marriage equality *(noun)*
The right of any two consenting adults to marry,
regardless of sex or gender

modern art (*noun*)
A style and period of art between the late 19th and the late 20th centuries that rejected traditional techniques of the past in the spirit of experimentation

print (*noun*)
A picture or design printed from a block or plate

sculpture (*noun*)
The art of making a three-dimensional forms

skein (*noun*)
A loosely coiled length of yarn

studio (*noun*)
A room where an artist works

tapestry (*noun*)
A thick piece of fabric with woven pictures or designs

Amy Guglielmo

Amy Guglielmo is an author, artist, arts educator, and arts advocate. She has written many books for children, including *Cezanne's Parrot* and *Just Being Dali: The Story of Artist Salvador Dali*. Amy has co-authored the picture books *Pocket Full of Colors: The Magical World of Mary Blair*, winner of the Christopher Award; *How to Build a Hug: Temple Grandin and Her Amazing Squeeze Machine*; and the *Touch the Art* series of novelty board books featuring famous works of art with tactile additions. She lives on Lake Champlain with her husband.

Katy Knapp

Originally from Norfolk, Katy Knapp moved to Brighton to study illustration at The University of Brighton and graduated in 2018. She now works as an illustrator from her seaside home in beautiful Hove. When she is not working, she likes drawing in her sketchbook in museums, singing along to musical theater soundtracks as loud as she can, and going on adventures to new places. Katy is passionate about telling the stories of incredible women through her work, so could not be more excited to be illustrating Louise's story.

Project Editor Rosie Peet
Project Art Editor Jon Hall
Art Director Clare Baggaley
Picture Researchers Martin Copeland,
Taiyaba Khatoon, and Aditya Katyal
Production Editor Siu Yin Chan
Production Controller Louise Minihane
Senior Acquisitions Editor Katy Flint
Managing Art Editor Vicky Short
Publishing Director Mark Searle

First American Edition, 2022
Published in the United States by DK Publishing
1450 Broadway, Suite 801, New York, NY 10018

Page design copyright © 2022 Dorling Kindersley Limited
DK, a Division of Penguin Random House LLC
22 23 24 25 26 10 9 8 7 6 5 4 3 2 1
001–327546–May/2022

The Metropolitan
Museum of Art
New York

A catalog record for this book
is available from the Library of Congress.
ISBN 978-0-7440-5469-9

DK books are available at special discounts when purchased in bulk for sales
promotions, premiums, fund-raising, or educational use.
For details, contact: DK Publishing Special Markets,
1450 Broadway, Suite 801, New York, NY 10018
SpecialSales@dk.com

Printed and bound in Latvia

Acknowledgments
DK would like to thank Lisa Silverman Meyers, Laura Corey,
Clare Davies, and Morgan Pearce at The Met; Maggie Wright and
Sewon Kang at The Easton Foundation; Hilary Becker; Clare Baggaley;
Jennette ElNaggar for proofreading; Amy Guglielmo and Katy Knapp.
The author would like to thank her partners in art,
Julie, Jacqueline, and Julia.

For the curious

www.dk.com
www.metmuseum.org

Sources for quotations

Page 28: Louise Bourgeois, "Self-Expression Is Sacred and Fatal," in Christiane Meyer-Thoss, *Louise Bourgeois: Designing for Free Fall*. Zurich: Ammann Verlag, 1992, p. 178

Page 31: Louise Bourgeois, *Ode à Ma Mère*. Paris: Les Éditions du Solstice, 1995, p. 9.

Page 37: Freedom to Marry. "Sale of Exclusive Art Edition Will Support the Campaign to Win Marriage Nationwide." Press release, May 11, 2010. www.freedomtomarry.org/blog/entry/louise-bourgeois-edition-to-benefit-freedom-to-marry

Page 39: "Artist Louise Bourgeois reveals her thoughts on drawing" *The Guardian*, September 18, 2009, www.theguardian.com/artanddesign/2009/sep/19/louise-bourgeois-on-drawing

Page 40: Louise Bourgeois, "Child Abuse: A Project by Louise Bourgeois." ARTFORUM (December 1982); p. 43

Page 42: Louise Bourgeois in conversation with Cecilia Blomberg, October 16, 1998, and quoted in "Spider," in Frances Morris, ed., *Louise Bourgeois*. London: Tate Modern, 2007, p. 272.

Page 44: Angela Doland, "Again, Bourgeois opens herself up." *Los Angeles Times*, March 24, 2008. www.latimes.com/archives/la-xpm-2008-mar-24-et-bourgeois24-story.html

Page 47: Paulo Herkenhoff, "Louise Bourgeois, Femme-Temps," in Asbaghi, Pandora Tabatabai, and Jerry Gorovoy, *Louise Bourgeois: Blue Days and Pink Days*. Italy: Fondazione Prada, 1997, p. 268.

Picture credits

The publisher would like to thank the following for their kind permission to reproduce their photographs:

(Key: a-above; b-below/bottom; c-centre; f-far; l-left; r-right; t-top)

40: Louise Bourgeois, *Femme Maison*, 1946–47. Oil and ink on linen. 36 × 14 in. (91.4 × 35.6 cm). Photo: Christopher Burke. © The Easton Foundation/VAGA at ARS, NY and DACS, London 2022 (cl); **Louise Bourgeois**, *The Sweet Smell of Indigo*, 1968. Watercolor, charcoal, and gouache on paper. 19 ¼ × 25 in. (48.9 × 63.5 cm). Collection Metropolitan Museum of Art, New York. Photo: Eeva Inkeri. © The Easton Foundation/VAGA at ARS, NY and DACS, London 2022 (cr). **41: Louise Bourgeois**, *Eyes*, 1982. Marble. 73 ¾ × 54 × 45 ¾ in. (187.3 × 137.2 × 116.2 cm). Collection Metropolitan Museum of Art, New York. Photo: Peter Bellamy. © The Easton Foundation/VAGA at ARS, NY and DACS, London 2022. **42: Louise Bourgeois**, *Three Horizontals*, 1998. Fabric and steel. 53 × 72 × 36 in. (134.6 × 182.8 × 91.4 cm). Photo: Christopher Burke. © The Easton Foundation/VAGA at ARS, NY and DACS, London 2022. **43: Louise Bourgeois**, *Maman*, 1999. Bronze, stainless steel, and marble. 365 × 351 × 403 in. (927.1 × 891.5 × 1023.6 cm). Photo: Marcus Leith. © The Easton Foundation/VAGA at ARS, NY and DACS, London 2022 (t); **Louise Bourgeois**, *Spider Woman*, 2005. Drypoint. 13 ½ × 13 ½ in. (34.3 × 34.3 cm). Photo: Christopher Burke. © The Easton Foundation/VAGA at ARS, NY and DACS, London 2022 (br).

All other images © Dorling Kindersley